10

A WRIGLEY BOOK

about

IDEAS

BY DENIS WRIGLEY

I'm not thinking of <u>anything</u>.

I __am__ thinking.

This is a picture of what
I am thinking.

It's a wonderful, colourful
pattern.

Now I am
thinking of the same
pattern.

I think it's wonderful too.

Thinking is using my brain.

I like using my brain.

Tell me something else
to think about.

Think of a door.

I am thinking of a door.

I am using my brain to think of a door.

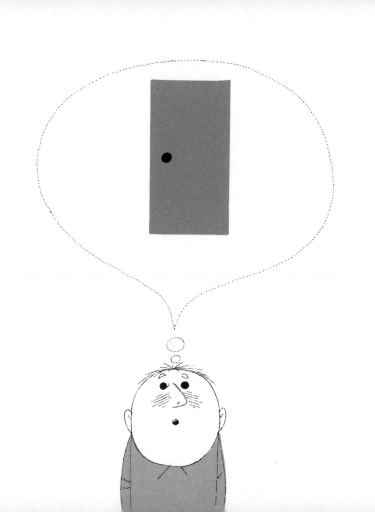

Now think of a key.

I am thinking of a door
and a key.

Think of a keyhole.

I am thinking of a key and a door and a keyhole.

Or I'm thinking of a keyhole
and a key and a door.

Or I'm thinking of a door,
a keyhole
and a key.

Now suppose
that the key fitted into
the keyhole
and unlocked
the door!

That's marvellous—
it's an idea!

I've thought of an idea....
AN IDEA!

When you think
about things......

and make them mean something

then you have an idea.

Think of some good ideas
of your own!

then you have an idea.

Think of some good ideas
of your own!

First published 1973
Copyright © 1973 Denis Wrigley
ISBN 0 7188 1938 1
Printed in Great Britain by
Redwood Press Limited
Trowbridge, Wiltshire

The Wrigley Books

Published by
LUTTERWORTH PRESS · GUILDFORD AND LONDON